It's Complicated

A Bible Study for Better Relationships

Eric B Summers

It's Complicated: A Bible Study for Better Relationships
Copyright © 2025 by Eric B Summers

ISBN: 978-1-968112-93-6

Printed in USA

Table of Contents

Chapter One: First Things First

This book is not intended to be a dating book, instead I felt called to speak to a bigger need and that is to help believers build bombproof relationships in their lives. This includes relationships with family members, with friends, and eventually significant others. There are concepts that can apply across all those relationships and fostering healthy relationships in our lives will help us all live a life that better honors God. Following the pandemic, our culture has struggled to get back to healthy relationships. Loneliness has skyrocketed and you can all agree that interactions with other humans hasn't gotten back to where it was pre-Covid. People are more distant, less kind, less loving. Relationships are struggling and the voices of culture don't know what to do about it. Thankfully we have a resource that stands the test of time and pandemic and that's the Bible. In this book we are going to look at Biblical examples of quality relationships and work through some practical ways for us to put these concepts into practice right away. If you are wanting a book on dating, this book will address some of the groundwork for you, but by design it's aimed at a larger topic.

I have been blessed with three amazing kids and with the help of my wife, we have navigated the dating world several times over. Instead of looking at dating as an isolated behavior, we have gone to Scripture to help our kids see their value, protect their hearts, and build quality circles of friends. Those lessons spill over into dating. We have had some victories as well as some failures along the way, but in all of it, we keep our eyes on Jesus. I hope the next couple of chapters will help you see your value as God sees it and build meaningful relationships that enrich the circles where God has planted you.

As we get into the opening section of this topic, I want to share a quote I found when I was studying for this book. There was an old pastor, Wilbert Gough, dude lived to 104, who gave this great advice,

> "Being the right person is as important as finding the right person."

Often, we focus so much on the other person that we forget to be the person we need to be in the relationship. Usually when you have a talk about relationships, it will start with Green Flags and Red Flags in the other person, but looking at Scripture, the real talk starts somewhere much closer to our hearts. It starts with us making sure we are the people we need to be before we can even hope to connect with another person. This means that we are living in a right relationship with God, growing in our love for Him, and an understanding of His heart for us. It has nothing to do with the other person and everything to do with us. When we take the time to be sure we are who we need to be, God will in His time introduce us to those other people. We can't skip that step of being who we need to be first.

As we open this discussion, we need to remember that God is involved in our relationships just like every other area of our life. He knows the desires of our hearts, and He knows how bad we want to find the right people in our lives. **Psalm 38:9** reminds us that *"O Lord, all my longing is before You; my sighing is not* *hidden from you.*" God knows our hearts desires, and He doesn't want our relationships to confuse us or cause emotional pain. So, we need to be sure we are in God's will for our lives as we start thinking about relationships. **Romans 12:2** is a great truth for us to apply here. "*Do not be conformed to this world, but be transformed by the renewal of your mind, that by testing you may discern what is the will of God, what is good and acceptable and perfect.*"

We need to focus more on God's plan and less on the voice of the culture around us. I want to clarify something that often gets overlooked in culture and that's the beauty of being single. Now this does apply more to dating relationships but can totally apply to our other relationships too. There is a big difference between alone and lonely. For some reason, everything pushes you to date. Somehow, being single is seen as a failure or that something is fundamentally wrong with you. This is not the case. There are so many different reasons to be single and many of them are actually very healthy.

Paul was a single guy, if he had been married, would he have been able to go on the missionary trips he took, would Mrs. Paul have been okay with him taking a stand for Jesus that constantly landed him in jail or in trouble with the law? Probably not. Paul's singleness was a gift and allowed him to be what God needed him to be. In **Philippians 4:11**, Paul tells the reader that he has learned to be content in whatever circumstance he has found himself in, that includes singleness. But I love how detailed the Holy Spirit was as He inspired Paul to write this letter. Paul "learned" how to be content. It was not the natural emotion for him.

If you are single right now, it's for a reason, don't think you are broken or unlovable. God has a purpose for this season and while there might be things you are working on, the same can be said for the person God will eventually introduce you to when the time is right In His Plan. I know from my own experience that even as a Christian, we often get so focused on finding the right people that we completely ignore our own development. We look for the person that makes us happy, which is a great trait, but we can never rely on another person for happiness, that comes from our relationship with God. When we put all that on another person, we are putting undue stress on the relationship, stress that we can't even live up to on our own end. So, my opening thought on the matter of relationships is that God wants us to be focused on our relationship with Him and trust in His time He will introduce us to the people who have been developing their relationships with Him in their own walk. When we rush ahead of that plan and take matters into our own hands, is when we run into all kinds of issues and heartbreak.

Chapter Two: Pick up your own stuff

Being the right person starts with presenting yourself to God. Read **Romans 12:1**, use the NLT as part of the reading on this one too. *"I appeal to you therefore, brothers, by the mercies of God, to present your bodies as a living sacrifice, holy and acceptable to God, which is your spiritual worship."*

We must surrender our entire life to God, including our relationships and all the desires that go with that. The problem with giving our lives as sacrifices is that we often take it back. We don't see God move as fast as we want or in the way we want, and we assume He is distant or uninterested in the wants of our heart, so we take over. Usually with bad results. We get so preoccupied with finding the people we are supposed to be with, we ignore what God wants from us. We hijack **Matthew 6:33** and force our relationships into the frame of that verse. *"But seek first the kingdom of God and his righteousness, and all these things will be added to you."*

We pray to God for an answer on who to date or who to let in our circles, when in fact this verse is really telling us to lay down all those other concerns and be content in God. Then in His time, He will give us what we need. **Psalm 37:4** is a great verse when it comes to building relationships and how all-consuming that process feels sometimes. *"Delight yourself in the Lord, and he will give you the desires of your heart."* When we delight in God and His daily presence in our lives, our wants will start to be more in line with His plan for our lives. When we stop looking at the cute girl/boy at church and wondering if they could be "the one," and instead focus on our connection to God, there we will find contentment and fulfillment. When we get those out of order, we will find frustration and pain.

Why is it so hard to look past "dating" and instead focus on our relationship with God? How does culture impact how much you focus on finding "the one?" Do you think you will find "the one" as a middle or even high schooler? It's rare, but possible to marry a childhood sweetheart. What kind of timeline do you see when it comes to dating? Is there an age you must be engaged/married? Do you have a "best-by" date when it comes to emotions? How can we be sure dating doesn't cause us to take our eyes off God? Can dating or even the pursuit of dating become an idol in our lives? What makes something an idol?

Integrity Matters

Character is a big deal! What kind of person are you looking for to be part of your life? Are they lazy, are they selfish, are they untrustworthy? Probably not, so flip that page over, are you the kind of person that someone is looking for. You need to be sure that your life measures up to the standard you are looking for in relationships as well!

Think about a house. Follow me here...what's the most important part? **The foundation**, did you get that? What do most people spend the most money on? **The finishes**. If the foundation is bad, what happens to the fancy kitchen and movie room? They fall apart. Our life is the same way, before we start putting on the fancy finishes, we must be sure the foundation is solid and that foundation must be built on God. Jesus teaches that truth using a story in **Matthew 7:24-26**. "*Everyone then who hears these words of mine and does them will be like a wise man who built his house on the rock. And the rain fell, and the floods came, and the winds blew and beat on that house, but it did not fall, because it had been founded on the rock. And everyone who hears these words of mine and does not do them will be like a foolish man who built his house on the sand.*" **What** does this say about our lives? What does it say about our relationships? As I read this story, I thought about all the things the world tells us to look for in others and how most of those things are "sand."

What are some "rock" things when it comes to relationships? Another way to ask that, what are some non-negotiables when it comes to allowing people into your life? This question will work for any age because even students who aren't ready to date still hear what they are to look for from siblings, family members, media, and friends.

Chapter Three: Boundaries

Last chapter we talked about how we need to be sure we are the kind of people we need to be before we ever start thinking about sharing life with someone else. We talked about how we need to have a right relationship with God first and how we need to be growing in that relationship. We also talked about how we need to be people of integrity before we ever start looking to share our life with another person. Parts of this series will lodge in your brain and when that day comes that you are dating, little nuggets of Scripture will pop back up and help you, it's how Scripture works. But even more immediate, all that have talked about can be applied to friendships and even family relationships. Relationship talks usually focus on the other person and we ignore our own shortcomings. So, I wanted to start off in the most important place, the only place we have some control, our relationship with God.

Boundaries are so important in relationships. I think most of the boundaries we have in life can be narrowed down to three main categories. Protecting our heart, protecting our circle, and protecting our name. Let's look at **Proverbs 4:23**.

> *"Keep your heart with all vigilance,*
> *for from it flow the springs of life."*

Solomon was called the wisest man in history, and he recognized the importance of protecting your heart. If that wasn't enough, turn to **Luke 6:43-45** and let's see what Jesus has to say about it. *"For no good tree bears bad fruit, nor again* *does a bad tree bear good fruit, for each tree is known by its own fruit. For figs are not gathered from thornbushes, nor are grapes picked from a bramble bush. The good person out of the good treasure of his heart produces good, and the evil person out of his evil treasure produces evil, for out of the abundance of the heart his mouth speaks."*

Jesus says that we will be known by the fruit of our lives and that fruit comes out of what is in our hearts. If we have compromised and allowed evil things to take root in our hearts, then our relationships and friendships will be marked with bad fruit. We will constantly have drama and insecurities. When we have put boundaries in place to keep bad things out of our hearts, we will find good fruit in our relationships with others. Things like joy, peace, and encouragement.

The second thing we need to protect is our circle. There are so many great truths in the Bible about our friends and choosing them carefully. **1 Corinthians 15:33** comes to mind quickly. *"Do not be deceived: "Bad company ruins good morals."* Paul wrote this truth to a church surrounded by an evil culture and the church was struggling to separate itself from those bad choices. This verse reminds us that when we surround ourselves with people making bad choices, we will surely start making bad choices ourselves. As we talk about protecting the circle of people around us, we need to put some distance between us and those consistently making bad choices. Another great truth we find from Solomon again in **Proverbs 13:20**. *"Whoever walks with the wise becomes wise, but the companion of fools will suffer harm."*

When we have wise people in our circle, our own decision making will start to mirror their wisdom. Not to say we will always get it right, but even when we start to make those dumb decisions, wise friends in our circles will call us out. As we talk about boundaries in our lives, we need to put boundaries around the people we let close to us to be sure they are sharpening us into the people we need to be and not pulling us away from God and His plan for us.

Finally, we need to protect our name. We need to have boundaries in our lives that protect our name or another way of saying that is our reputation. **Proverbs 22:1** reminds us that our name is more valuable than great riches. *"A good name is to be chosen rather than great riches, and favor is better than silver or gold."*

If we allow people to tear down our name or if we make choices that smudges our name, we are sacrificing far more than we think. We don't want friends around us that talk about us behind our backs, and we also don't want our actions to cause other people to doubt our relationship with God. Both of those actions will ruin our name. **Proverbs 10:7** is a harsh reminder of how important our reputation is. *"The memory of the righteous is a blessing, but the name of the wicked will rot."*

When we live a God-honoring life, our lives will be a blessing to others. When we live our lives honoring our selfish desires, our name will be rotten to the those around us. Protecting our name is important. Does this mean that we should chase down every person spreading false rumors about us and pummel them to the ground? No, not really the right way to handle that either. People will always talk, and shallow insecure people will put others down to make themselves feel more important. **1 Peter 2:12** reminds us to keep our conduct honorable so that **WHEN** they speak ill against us, people will know their words are empty.

All three of the areas we talked about need our attention and protection. We must be aware of threats to our heart, our circles, and our name. These threats are just as dangerous in friendships as they are in dating relationships. You can't expect to have bad fruit in your friendships and then a super healthy dating relationship. Your friendships are a proving ground for the boundaries you will put in place in your dating life. If you are seeing bad fruit in your friendships, you really need to do some work personally before you even start to date, or you will see the same kind of bad fruit there as well. I think our friendships are more important and require our attention before who we are going to date. If our friendships are off, then of course our dating relationship will be off too. Scripture gives us some great boundaries regarding our relationships with others; we just have to put them into practice.

Chapter Four: Protect These Things

Protect Your Heart

Philippians 4:6-7

"Do not be anxious about anything, but in everything by prayer and supplication with thanksgiving let your requests be made known to God. And the peace of God, which surpasses all understanding, will guard your hearts and your minds in Christ Jesus."

Psalm 51:10

*"Create in me a clean heart, O God,
and renew a right spirit within me"*

Proverbs 7:25

*"Let not your heart turn aside to her ways;
do not stray into her paths"*

Matthew 6:21

"For where your treasure is, there your heart will be also."

Matthew 15:18

"But what comes out of the mouth proceeds from the heart, and this defiles a person."

Matthew 22:37

"And he said to him, "You shall love the Lord your God with all your heart and with all your soul and with all your mind."

These are just a few verses that deal with our heart, what's in it, and how to protect it. What are some big picture things you take away from these verses about how your heart is at risk in relationships?

Would it be easier to just keep everyone at a distance? No, we are built to live in community with others, we must open our hearts to other people. Who we open it to and how much we allow in are up to us. Those factors are how we protect our heart.

Take the dating piece off for a second, what kind of things are you letting in your heart that are bad for it? What media are you consuming that influence your emotions in a negative way? What advice are you listening to from others that might not be in the best interest of your heart? What lies are you believing on social media that make your heart long for things it doesn't really need? Are you keeping a friend who thrives on drama close out of ease instead of having a tough conversation?

Protect Your Circle

Next in priority is looking carefully at the people around you. If you are surrounded by people chasing after their own things at the cost of everyone else, you will find those behaviors creeping into your life as well. Friendships and relationships should never be entered with the intent of changing the other person. In the first place that is terribly arrogant to think you know the best version of that other person, but on the flip side, you would find yourself more impacted by their bad behaviors than improved by your good attempts.

Here are some passages about protecting your circle:

Proverbs 27:17

"Iron sharpens iron, and one man sharpens another."

John 15:13

"Greater love has no one than this, that someone lay down his life for his friends."

Ecclesiastes 4:9-12

"Two are better than one, because they have a good reward for their toil. For if they fall, one will lift up his fellow. But woe to him who is alone when he falls and has not another to lift him up! Again, if two lie together, they keep warm, but how can one keep warm alone?"

Proverbs 27:6

"Faithful are the wounds of a friend; profuse are the kisses of an enemy."

Romans 12:10

"Love one another with brotherly affection. Outdo one another in showing honor."

Why is our circle of friends so important to the kind of person we become? Why do people spend so much time and energy trying to impress other people that don't share their beliefs or priorities? In protecting our circles, should we only have "church people" in our circles? No, we should all have lost friends, but we need to understand their thought process will be different. We still love them, and we seek to show through our actions and our words, the love of Jesus to them.

What are some boundaries you can put into place for the people you let close to you? What are behaviors you should distance yourself from? How can you compassionately move someone outside of your circle when you recognize they aren't someone who should be in your closest circle? How does popularity tie into this point? What happens when your dating relationship pushes away your quality friendships?

Protect Your Name

Finally, we want to talk about protecting your reputation. This isn't about keeping up appearances or facades, this is about making sure you are living in a way that points the world to Jesus. There are way too many people in the church that are more concerned about what other people think of them instead of what God thinks of them. They have misunderstood the call to protect their name. Your name is more than your profile picture or social media image. Your name is comprised of the choices you make, the priorities you keep, the service you give others, and the humility you demonstrate. There was no such thing as "influencers" in the Bible, that's a modern concept where people pick and choose what parts of their life they show. Only picking the best parts to make them look great. There was a group of people that Jesus often bumped heads with that were more concerned with appearances than the depth of their character, the religious leaders, the Pharisees. He continually calls out their hypocrisy. When we talk about protecting our name. It's not about our image, but our character.

Here are some verses that speak to that:

Matthew 5:16

"In the same way, let your light shine before others, so that they may see your good works and give glory to your Father who is in heaven."

1 Peter 2:11-12

"Beloved, I urge you as sojourners and exiles to abstain from the passions of the flesh, which wage war against your soul.[12] Keep your conduct among the Gentiles honorable, so that when they speak against you as evildoers, they may see your good deeds and glorify God on the day of visitation."

Philippians 1:27

"Only let your manner of life be worthy[a] of the gospel of Christ, so that whether I come and see you or am absent, I may hear of you that you are standing firm in one spirit, with one mind striving side by side for the faith of the gospel"

1 Timothy 4:12

"Let no one despise you for your youth, but set the believers an example in speech, in conduct, in love, in faith, in purity."

Titus 2:6-8

"Likewise, urge the younger men to be self-controlled. Show yourself in all respects to be a model of good works, and in your teaching show integrity, dignity, and sound speech that cannot be condemned, so that an opponent may be put to shame, having nothing evil to say about us."

In your own words, what is the difference between keeping up appearances and protecting your character? People are going to slander you regardless of how good you are, what are things you just let slide and what things do you address? How can protecting your name play into a dating relationship? What if people say you passed physical boundaries that you haven't, how does that impact your name? What if someone falsely accuses you of cheating, how does that impact your name? Then how do those accusations reflect on your claim to be "in Christ?"

Chapter Five: Your Value

As we think about relationships and specifically dating relationships, what is the most important date on the dating calendar every year? **Valentines Day.** Which is supposed to be a romantic day for everyone right...but we all know that doesn't always play out that way. There are plenty of single people on Valentines Day, a day when all media and marketing remind us of how good it is to be in a relationship. This is the perfect day to talk about how much God loves us. Now I know that sounds super cheesy and super "churchy", but it's true. Scripture is crammed full of valentines from God reassuring you of just how much you are loved. Your creator loves you tremendously and even though the voices of the world try to tell you otherwise, He wants you to know just how much He loves you. Let's look at some of those love letters in the Bible together.

Let's start in Psalms as we look at some aspects of God's love for us. **Psalm 36:5-7** shows us how big God's love for us is.

> "Your steadfast love, O Lord, extends to the heavens,
> your faithfulness to the clouds.
> Your righteousness is like the mountains of God;
> your judgments are like the great deep;
> man and beast you save, O Lord.
> How precious is your steadfast love, O God!
> The children of mankind take refuge in the shadow of your wings."

It reaches far and wide and it protects us from harm like a bird protects it's young with its wings. I'm an old school nerd so when I think of God's love protecting us under His wings, I think less of the forest scene and more of an Xmen image with Archangel protecting a teammate. Seems more powerful to my mind and the imagery inside my head. But whatever works for you on the imagery.

In **Psalm 31:7** we are told that God's love is there for us when we are going through a hard time.

" I will rejoice and be glad in your steadfast love,
because you have seen my affliction;
you have known the distress of my soul"

We can rejoice in the hard time because we know that God has seen our suffering and as a loving Father, is working things out for our good as Scripture promises. Does that mean we don't suffer? No, it means we have a God that isn't distant or happy about our suffering. Instead, God lovingly works to comfort and deliver us. God's love is unique to each of us. It's personal, He knows us individually and loves us that way. **1 John 3:1** says that He loves us so much, we are called children of God. A good father knows his children, he knows their actions, their habits, and their hearts. Our God is the perfect father, and He knows more about us than anyone else on the earth. He loves us personally, not just as a group of followers. Maybe some of the most powerful reminders of God's love are found in Romans and Ephesians as we hear a little more about the kind of love God has for us. **Romans 5:8** is a verse I often recite to myself when I'm struggling with my worth. *"But God shows his love for us in that while we were still sinners, Christ died for us."*

It tells us that God's love extended to us when we were at our lowest state. We didn't have to clean ourselves up first or follow all the rules. God loved us in our brokenness. **Ephesians 2:4-5** echoes that idea as it reminds us that God sent Jesus to save us, while we were undeserving and actively rebelling against Him. *"But God, being rich in mercy, because of the great love with which he loved us, even when we were dead in our trespasses, made us alive together with Christ—by grace you have been saved "*

It's easy to love people that are nice to you, it's another thing all together to love people that are against you. That's what Romans 5 and Ephesians 2 is saying to us. God loved us when we were enemies and sent Jesus to save each of us from the result of that horrible lifestyle. **Ephesians 3:18-19** tells us another great thing about God's love for us, and that it will be hard for us to understand. His love is too much for us to understand, because we only have the kind of love we have experienced in this life. Very few things if anything in this life, comes close to the love that God has for us.

What is God's love for us like? Scripture uses the Greek word "Agape" which is a specific kind of love. In Greek, the language the NT is written in, the word we use for "love" had four different words, each with its own meaning and context. Today we "love" a lot of things. We love the new song from the artist we like, we "love" our favorite kind of pizza, we "love" our dog, and we "love" our family...even though we only like them sometimes. How can one word convey all the emotions that I just mentioned? It doesn't do it well, saying you love a specific food and saying you love your best friend puts them on the same level when we all understand you love your friend in a much more meaningful way. You might be sad if that dish comes off the menu, but you would be heartbroken if your friend had to move away.

Simply saying we love something doesn't accurately convey the emotions involved. That's why I like how the Greek's did it. They had four words for love: Agape, Phileo, Eros, and Storge are the most common. **Storge** is family love. The kind of love that you have towards parents or siblings. We always say in our family that I will always love you, but I don't always have to like you. While we are joking a little, storge love is that kind of feeling. Family will always be family, even if it's not blood related. **Eros** is the mushy kind of love that is between a romantic couple, it focuses on physical demonstrations and is what most people think of around Valentine's Day. **Phileo** is the love that we have for our closest friends. It's a brotherly love where we care about a person, their wellbeing, and we want them in our circles.

Finally, we have **Agape,** and this love is unconditional and probably the only relationship that comes close to this in our lives is that love that a parent has for their children. Now I know every family dynamic is different and sometimes the love between parents and kids is tough. But most every other relationship we have in this life is dependent on how the other person treats us as to how we feel about them. That's conditional love and thankfully, that's not how God loves us. His love for us isn't confined to those days when we are following the rules well or reading our Bible's regularly.

We looked at a few passages earlier that told us that God loves us in our brokenness and even sent Jesus when we were still enemies with Him. What that tells me is that there is nothing I can do our not do, that will change the way God loves me. In our Heavenly Father's eyes, we are worth more than the life of Jesus, Scripture tells us that is the price that was paid. And He loves us with a love so big and so counter cultural, that Scripture tells us we can't even understand it all. I'm thankful that God loves me that much and while I have some great examples in love around me in this life...to know that God still loves me more...makes even the best Valentine's Day seem small. So remember that you are each loved with an unconditional love by the God who created you!

Chapter Six: Finding Value

Where do YOU find your value...

Right off the bat we are going to brainstorm about what gives us our value, you might have some "church" answers in your head, but I imagine you have lots of other factors too. Everyone is different. I'm going to give you some space to write here. Now before I upset anyone, I'm particular about how I keep my paper books and IF I let someone borrow a book of mine, I'm super careful to explain my expectations with my book to them. I have had students borrow my books and when it came time to bring it back realize they didn't take care of it to my standard, and they bought a brand-new book to return to me. I do take notes in my books where it's meaningful, but I'm super careful with everything else. No bent corners and I do my best not to crease the spine. If you are like me and don't want to mess this book up, feel free to use an index card that you can slide into the book later to write down where you find your value. If you are one of those people whose books look like a dog chewed on them, go ahead and write down where you found your value in this box below.

What do we need to avoid when it comes to our value...

Comparison: One of the biggest thieves of our own value is comparison with other people. Social media only makes this worse. People put their best foot forward, even if totally made up, and then you compare yourself to their fictional self. One of the Scriptures we looked at in the opening reminded us that God knows us personally. **1 John 3:1** tells us that God loves us and calls us His children. He is our biggest supporter and loves us more than we can know. He doesn't compare us to other people; He loves us individually! **Jeremiah 1:5** is a great reminder of this.

> "Before I formed you in the womb I knew you,
> and before you were born, I consecrated you;
> I appointed you a prophet to the nations."

Success: Another thing to look out for is letting our success tell us our worth. When we are on the winning team, it's easy to think we are doing good. When we are losing, how do we feel about ourselves? At those moments we must think about the variables that are in our control. If it's a sporting event, we are one person on a team of many, we can only do our best and trust that everyone else is doing the same. We can't pin our value to the success of the team when there are so many variables at play. The same goes for school/work. There are times when we are going to do our best, crushing the task we had been given, and in the end, the group won't succeed. We can't let those moments define our worth. This isn't an excuse, it's a method of framing your thoughts to be more Biblical. We never want to pass blame, but we also can't take the blame for someone else's actions.

Friends: We have talked numerous times about the importance of your circle. The people you keep close and let into your heart. Friends will usually encourage you, but sometimes they can tear you down too. In those times, it's important for us to realize that even our friends don't set our worth. As awesome as they may be, they are working through their own things and own insecurities. Sometimes the stuff they are dealing with will spill over onto us. We need to know our worth separate of what our friends say about us. **Romans 12:9-10** tells us the best way to build up our friends, while also warning us to stay away from negative habits.

> *"Let love be genuine. Abhor what is evil; hold fast to what is good. Love one another with brotherly affection. Outdo one another in showing honor."*

Boyfriend/Girlfriend: Too many people allow a significant other to make them feel a certain way about themselves. They can make you feel very special, or they can make you feel like nobody else would ever want you. When you give too much power to a significant other, you are opening yourself up to false statements about your worth. Manipulation will find its way into a relationship and one person might belittle the other person to keep them under control because they don't understand their own worth to begin with. This isn't healthy and this isn't God's design for us. There is a certain boundary you keep on your heart until you are married, regardless of how long you have been dating or how "in love" you are. Until you have made the commitment to do life together...forever...you protect your heart and your worth even from the one you are dating. In **1 Corinthians 13: 4-7**, Paul lays out what God-honoring love looks like. It's a list of characteristics...if you don't see these in your dating life, you should have a red flag about that relationship.

Since we are talking about knowing our worth in the relationships we have here on Earth, it's important to know how we receive and give love to others. Gary Chapman is famous for writing the book that outlines the 5 Love Languages. Gary's idea is that we all have a love tank in our lives. We receive love into this tank, and we pour love out of this tank. Think of it like a gas tank on the car. If we keep driving and pouring out love to other people and never receive love from anyone...what happens? We run out of gas, the car stops going, and we are broken inside. So, while it's important to show love to others, it's also important that we continually fill up that tank as we go. An early chapter in the book talks about knowing your love language, the way you receive love the best. What shows your friend you love them, might not work the same for you. Gary outlines 5 main languages: *Quality Time, Physical Touch, Words of Affirmation, Acts of Service, and Giving of Gifts.*

There are several online tests for you to take on your own time to get an idea of what your love language is. I challenge you to have your close friends also take the test and then share with each other. It's crucial to a good relationship to give and receive love in an effective and meaningful way.

Chapter Seven: Watch the Flags

I have one more piece of wisdom to pass down to you guys and that's the importance of identifying relationship flags. We have said just about every week that while these conversations can apply to dating relationships, it's better to apply them to all your relationships as you seek to protect your heart. You don't have to be dating someone to get hurt and you don't have to be dating to hurt someone else. You can all think of a friend who used to be close and through some communication issue you guys aren't as close now. It's important to recognize the flags in our lives.

In Paul's letter to the Corinthian church, we can pull some relationship flags from a great list. **1 Corinthians 13:4-7, 13**: *"Love is patient and kind; love does not envy or boast; it is not arrogant or rude. It does not insist on its own way; it is not irritable or resentful; it does not rejoice at wrongdoing but rejoices with the truth. Love bears all things, believes all things, hopes all things, endures all things."* **And** *"So now faith, hope, and love abide, these three; but the greatest of these is love"*

In Paul's letter to the church at Corinth, he gives a great description of what love looks like when it's lived out properly. We have already talked about the different words used in the Bible for love and how they have different meanings and level of love. Our English word is just kind of lame when it comes to really communicating love. So, you don't have to go back to your Greek New Testaments, I went ahead and looked up the Greek used in this passage and the type of love we are hearing here from Paul is "Agape" which is the unconditional kind of love that God shows towards us. This kind of love is incredibly hard for us to live out. Even the people we really care about can hurt us and we can pull away to protect our heart. That's a conditional love, but as we read 1 Corinthians 13, we know the Holy Spirit led Paul to write that specific kind of love into this verse. But we aren't just left with this unattainable bar of what love looks like, Paul gives us some practical things about this kind of love and how it's lived out.

Let's start with **Patience**. The kind of love we are supposed to have in all our relationships is a patient love. This means that we are slow to repay each other for wrongs. When someone does something that hurts you, it's natural to want to strike back, but patience delays those emotions and shows self-control. You value that relationship more than you value vengeance. It doesn't mean we just overlook it and act like a doormat letting everyone step on us, but we are slow to repay wrong.

Next is **Envy**. There is nothing wrong with admiring something about another person or something they have, but if that admiration turns into jealousy, it because a very toxic emotion. Jealousy is a fatal word in dating relationships and a horribly toxic trait in friendships. Social media and its false images of perfection don't help this attitude either. You see couples that look like every second they are awake is total bliss and become jealous of that. The reality is that they have curated that image, meaning it's made up. In friendships it's when you allow your friends success to make you jealous instead of being happy for them. That seed of jealousy will cause you to resent your friend and will slowly corrupt the friendship from the inside. **Philippians 2:3** reminds us to be humble in our relationships and keep jealousy far away. "*Do nothing from selfish ambition or conceit, but in humility count others more significant than yourselves.* "

The next attitude we hear about is **Arrogance**. What does that look like in relationships? As I worked through this passage, the word we see translated "arrogance" can also be read as "proud." To be prideful is to be overly self-confident. You think too much of yourself and that's not what Jesus modeled for us. **Proverbs 16:18** reminds us of what our pride leads to.

> *"Pride goes before destruction, and a haughty spirit before a fall."*

When pride is present in a relationship, that prideful person is too busy appreciating their own awesomeness and isn't building up the other person. They are selfish and most of the conversations end up being about them and their accomplishments. A good friendship and a good relationship bring value to both sides and both sides have equal voice. Part of the next verse builds off that in how love isn't self-seeking. This goes back to the concept of agape love.

People that love this way aren't in it for what they can get out of the relationship. They think of the other person more than themselves. This doesn't mean they don't stand up for themselves, it means that their wants are second priority. This was a big shock to the reader in the 1st century and continues to be one for us. Most everything we hear and see in our culture points to us getting what we want to be happy at any cost. Scripture tells us that true happiness is found in Jesus and lived out by serving others.

If you read the 1st Corinthians passage in a different translation, there is part that you might have been looking for in what we just read. In this ESV it's listed as a footnote and that part is that love **keeps no record of wrong**. This is perhaps one of the biggest things when it comes to our relationships and how to keep them God-honoring. Scripture is crystal clear that God forgives our sin when we ask Him to, and He casts it farther away than we can imagine. **Psalm 103:12**, but how does that translate to our relationships and how we offer forgiveness

We should do the same...right? But it's hard to forgive when we have been hurt by a friend. Even if we work past it over time, it's always sitting there in the back of our mind and if something close to that happens again, all those emotions come flaring back up again. The kind of love we are to practice in our friendships and when we date, is the kind that doesn't catalog all the mistakes that other person has made at some point in the past. I've heard a phrase so many times that says we are to always forgive but never forget wrongs. I think there is some good truth to this, and some troubling truth too. The idea of not ignoring when someone has wronged us is a good. When we withhold forgiveness, we are only hurting ourselves. But we also don't want to be naïve when a person's bad behaviors become a cycle that impacts us.

Look at the closing verses as they tell us some powerful things about that kind of love that we are to show in our relationships. Scripture tells us that love bears all things, believes all things, hopes all things, endures all things, and at the end it says that faith, hope, and love are all important, but love is the greatest. Love is a powerful thing and when lived out like God wants us to, it is beautiful and brings joy to both sides. Unfortunately, because of sin it's corruption of this world, there is a lot of hurt in this life at the hands of friends. In the next chapter, we are going to talk about some specific things to look out for that will contrast the things we just talked about. Everyone has unique hurts from friends and from dating, so we can't possibly hope to hit them all, but there are several red flags that we have all experienced in our relationships. Talking through those together will help us move past that hurt and will also help us be accountable to each other to not allow those attitudes to creep in our friendships

Chapter Eight: Red Flags

As we work through some of these red flags, it's much easier to see them in others than to recognize them in ourselves. Be sure we are being honest with ourselves and striving to rid these red flags and others from our own behaviors so that we are loving others like we are called to love them in Scripture. All drama has two sides.

Romans 12:18: *"If possible, so far as it depends on you, live peaceably with all."* What can you control when it comes to relationships and red flag behaviors?

Red Flag #1- Deception of any kind

There's simply nothing loving about being lied to or deceived. As **1 Corinthians 13:6-7** says: *"Love does not delight in evil but rejoices in the truth. It always protects, always trusts, always hopes, always perseveres."* Deception in relationships will undermine any sense of trust, which is a non-negotiable in any relationship. Is there any level of lie that is okay in a friendship/dating relationship? Is telling the truth always easy? What kind of behaviors should you look for early on when it comes to deception from a friend? Is there an area in your life where you find yourself taking the easy way out instead of being truthful with others?

Red Flag #2- All talk, no fruit

Matthew 7:18-19 tells us that a person's actions will tell us much more than their words. *"A healthy tree cannot bear bad* *fruit, nor can a diseased tree bear good fruit. Every tree that does not bear good fruit is cut down and thrown into the fire."*

When someone says that you are important to them, they will make time for you. When they are constantly making excuses, it's a sign to where you are at in their priorities. When someone says their faith is important to them, but then their lifestyle doesn't mirror that, they are putting on a facade, and that goes back to Red Flag #1. How can you tell if you are important to someone? How is it different between friends and boyfriend/girlfriends? What kind of behaviors let you know that you aren't a priority to someone? How do you distance yourself from that relationship? Are there people in your life that think you are closer than you really are?

Are you doing something to perpetuate that? Can you fix it?

Red Flag #3- Manipulation

Statistics show that 1 in 4 women and 1 in 7 men are in an abusive relationship or have been abused. Many of them either saw the signs ahead of time and ignored them. Why would anyone stay in a relationship with an abusive individual? Because they are repeatedly told by the abuser that it will never happen again or they become convinced they deserve the abuse and believe that if they leave the relationship, no one else will ever love them.

There are many types of abuse—physical, sexual, verbal, and emotional. We don't want to believe that someone who claims to love us would abuse us. But relationships can be manipulative. And abuse can be subtle.

If you have reservations about the abusive tendencies of your relationship, don't just consider breaking it off. Run. Anyone who repeatedly hurts you physically or emotionally needs professional help, not a relationship that enables them to continue their abusive or manipulative behavior. These stats are focused on dating, but manipulation and emotional abuse can happen in friendships as well. What does manipulation or abuse look like with friends? When we allow others to manipulate or abuse us, we are denying our God-given worth. How do we break away from a manipulative person? Think back to **Judges 16** and the story of Samson. Delilah was a manipulator. She wanted to know Samson's secret so she could tell his enemies. When he wouldn't tell her the truth, she started pulling on his heart strings and using his emotions to get the information she waned. Was Delilah working in Samson's best interest? Absolutely not. He caved to her manipulation and where did it take him? Do people that truly love you manipulate you?

Red Flag #4- Communication

This is a big deal in friendships and in relationships. Being able to communicate well on a regular basis is crucial to lasting connections with other people. Here are a few points from Scripture about how we communicate with others. **James 1:19** is a verse I always keep in my memory.

> *"Know this, my beloved brothers: let every person be quick to hear, slow to speak, slow to anger"*

It keeps my order of operations in check. Quick to hear means that I listen more than I talk. Slow to talk means I think through my words before they spill out of my lips. Words are like toothpaste, once it's out there, it's not going back in. And finally, being slow to anger means controlling my emotions when talking to someone else. I don't respond in the heat of the moment; emotions can affect what you hear and how you take those statements. So be sure you are in control of your emotions when communicating with others.

Ephesians 4:29 is another great verse about our words when communicating with others. *"Let no corrupting talk come out of your mouths, but only such as is good for building up, as fits the occasion, that it may give grace to those who hear."*

Our words should build each other up. How does that work in friendships? How do you build the other person up with your words in a dating relationship? On the flip side, how can your words ruin a friendship? How can a pattern of poor communication undermine a dating relationship? What is poor communication in a relationship?

\ **Proverbs 10:19** is a great passage about the words that come out of our mouths. In the Living Bible Translation, it says this, *"Don't talk so much. You keep putting your foot in your mouth. Be sensible and turn off the flow!"* This verse isn't telling us to not talk to other people; it's reminding us that sometimes we talk too much about unnecessary things and in those moments, we often say dumb things. Good communication is so important and there a bunch of red flags that are communication specific.

What are some things you have experienced where communication has failed in your relationships? Where do you see good communication modeled?

Red Flags

I reached out to my daughter to ask some of her friends and the students she tutors about red flags they see in relationships, and they came back with a full list. I share these as talking points, I'm sure many of our students have experienced the same things in their own lives.

►►►

"Talking" to more than one person

Calling ex's crazy (hating on the person, talking about it all the time)

Snapchat/social media is primary form of communication

Can't carry on a conversation

Blowing you off/canceling plans

Jealous/possessive (unhealthy way)

Guy doesn't pick girl up for first date (older high school)

Not motivated (life, school, career, sports, etc.)

Liar

Love bombing – you can Google this one if you need to.

Crossing boundaries

Not willing to have hard conversations (such as placing healthy boundaries)

Says they're going to change and don't

Unwilling to compromise

Victim mentality (everyone is out to get them)

Lack of communication/effort overall

Controlling

Manipulative

Lack of trust (taking and going through phone)

Having a bad/toxic friend group

Too clingy

Bad relationship with parents (guys who mistreat their moms and girls who mistreat their dads)

Unhealthy family dynamic

Conclusion

As we close this journey together, I want to remind you that relationships, while often messy and complicated, are one of the most powerful tools God uses to shape us. Whether it's our friendships, our family dynamics, or even romantic connections, each interaction gives us the chance to reflect the heart of Christ and grow in our understanding of His love. If we want strong, God-honoring relationships, it starts with our own foundation—our walk with Jesus. We've talked about boundaries, character, red flags, our value, and the importance of guarding our hearts. But none of those things work unless we surrender our lives to Christ daily and let Him guide us. Relationships don't flourish when we chase validation from others—they flourish when we rest in the truth that we are already deeply loved by our Creator.

So, as you leave these pages and return to your world—your friends, your family, your texts and socials—my challenge is this: Don't settle for what the world says relationships should be. Choose something better. Be the person God is calling you to be before worrying about who might walk into your life next. Build relationships that sharpen, encourage, and reflect the love and grace you've found in Jesus. The path may not always be easy, but it's worth it. And remember, when it comes to love, community, and connection—God isn't silent, and He certainly isn't absent. Trust Him to write your story. It may be complicated, but with Him, it's never without purpose.

About the Author

Eric Summers has served as a dedicated student pastor for over 20 years, walking alongside young people as they navigate faith, life, and purpose. Beyond the church walls, Eric is a committed husband and the proud father of three amazing children who continually inspire and challenge him to lead by example. An avid soccer coach and lifelong athlete, he brings the same energy and discipline to the field as he does to ministry. Eric is also an active member of the F3 fitness community and a passionate Rucker, always pushing himself and others to grow stronger—physically, mentally, and spiritually. Whether in the locker room, on the trail, or at the pulpit, Eric leads with heart, humility, and an unshakable belief in the power of **functional faith**.

Acknowledgments

This book wouldn't exist without the incredible grace and support of my family. To my wife—thank you for your constant encouragement, insight, and patience. You've been the anchor in every season, and your wisdom continues to shape how I see relationships and lead others well. To my kids—you've been the real-life lab partners in this journey. Watching you navigate friendships, dating, and the pressures of growing up has not only inspired this study but made it deeply personal. Thank you for the honest conversations, the laughs, and even the awkward moments—you've helped make this book what it is.

I'm also incredibly grateful for the strong, godly men God has placed in my life. To my fellow pastors, thank you for sharpening me, challenging me, and walking this road of ministry and discipleship side by side. And to my F3 brothers—you've shown me the power of male friendships rooted in accountability, faith, and grit. In the gloom, on the trails, and in the trenches, you've reminded me that we're always better together. This book is better because of all of you.